Behind The Chair

Memories, Thoughts, Lessons, And Blessings

Timmigo K. Burnett

~2 Corinthians 5:17~

Therefore if any man be in Christ, he is a new creature:
old things are passed away; behold, all things are become new.

Copyright © 2015 by Timmigo K. Burnett

Behind the Chair
Memories, Thoughts, Lessons, and Blessings
by Timmigo K. Burnett

Printed in the United States of America.

ISBN 9781498439206

Edited by Xulon Press

All rights reserved solely by the author. The author guarantees all contents are original and do not infringe upon the legal rights of any other person or work. No part of this book may be reproduced in any form without the permission of the author. The views expressed in this book are not necessarily those of the publisher.

Unless otherwise indicated, Scripture quotations taken from the King James Version (KJV). Copyright © 1988 by Thomas Nelson, Inc. Used by permission. All rights reserved.

www.xulonpress.com

Table of Contents

Foreword vii

Introduction ix

Dedication xiii

Acknowledgments xv

The Barber's History 17

The Barber's Pole 19

The Black Barbershop 26

Broken Home 29

My Foundation 34

Life's Work 39

Decision Time 42

Inside Pain 48

Each One Teach One 54

The Ride to Work 60

My Success 64

Lost Communication 69

Unnoticed Tears 73

Behind the Chair

The Last Time and Phone Calls 81
We Are all Handicapped 87
After the Program/After the Benediction 93
Tribute: Little Did I Know 98
A Poem for My Bride 101

Foreword
By
Dr. M. Keith McDaniel, Sr.
Pastor of Macedonia Missionary Baptist Church, Spartanburg, SC

The barbershop, a sacred place for men and boys. It is a place of fashion, family and fellowship. It is a safe place for men to gather, a sacred intuition in the rite of passage from boyhood to manhood. Many families celebrate the first haircut of a male toddler. It is a place where fathers spend time with their sons, where the latest trends are discussed, and it is a good place to get good advice.

The basketball court, the urban training ground for building character, developing a concept of teamwork and determination. It is a place of competition, power and speed. It is a place of physical activity, mental quickness and raw emotions. It is the one place where hoops, hopes and hops make sense when used in the same sentence.

The barbershop and the basketball court are two important stations of development in the life of most males. In this book, *Behind the Chair,* Timmigo Burnett invites us to journey through his lived experiences. It is a reflective work of growth and spiritual maturity. He proudly proclaims that God saved him, but basketball raised him. As a professional barber for over twenty-three years and a continued student of the game of basketball, God has allowed Timmigo to see life from a number of vantage points, all of which come to life in this written work.

A life without reflection is a life void of understanding. Reflection affords one the opportunity to examine perspective, and perspective is an amazing thing. Perspective is the unique quality that both skilled barbers and skilled basketball players share in common. What they see determines how they cut. Whether they are cutting to the basket or whether they are cutting hair, perspective is their guide.

Perspective shapes our attitude and our altitude. It forms our understanding of the past and gives us direction in shaping our vision for the future. What are you looking at? What are you looking for? Where are you looking from? As you read this work, allow Timmigo to guide you through his own life perspective. I am certain you will see your own life as he tells his journey from behind the chair.

Introduction

Even though this book is autobiographical, it does not follow a birth to present chronology. It is simply a thoughtful recollection of different stages in my growth.

I remember that morning vividly. It was February 4th, 2014. I arrived to work at 7:15 A.M. At first, I didn't understand what I was feeling. I imagine that this feeling was similar to what I have been told happens to those who are called into the ministry. I was standing at the back bar in the barbershop when God spoke to me. He said, "It's time for you to write that book." I had lots of answers for God, but I also had questions.

I asked, "What book?"

He answered, "The book that you're going to write, and you can tell somebody."

So, I called my wife, Sharon, and told her that God had instructed me to write a book. She said, "Huh, well…ok." At that point, I hung up the phone and looked in the mirror to continue my conversation

Behind the Chair

with God. As I said before, I had lots of questions, and I really wanted to do some negotiating with God. I thought we might be able to come to an agreement.

I continued, "Okay God, here I am. So what is the name of this book? I'm a busy man, and I don't have time to write a book." I tried to make excuses and give reasons why I could not do it.

God answered simply, "You will." I thought that if I had ever written a book about anything, it would be a fundamental basketball book, but this book wasn't it. I looked down and I was standing behind my barber's chair. My mouth fell open. I couldn't believe it. That's the name of the book: *Behind the Chair*. God had given me the title. The next question I had for God was what to write about. Again, He answered, "Write about memories, moments, events, thoughts, experiences, you, life lessons, and blessings. Make it clean, clean enough to be sold in any Christian bookstore." I was also instructed to insert a scripture at the end of each chapter.

I still asked God questions like how and where I should start in the book. "Do I write from beginning to the end? What do I do?" I inquired.

"No," God answered. "Start wherever you want to start: in the middle, at the end, or at the beginning. You will be able to put the chapters where they belong when you complete the book. Write it your way. This is your book."

What was I to do? I said, "God, I don't know many scriptures. I'll have to consult my pastor every time I need a scripture." The answer

Introduction

came clearly to me again. Everything about life has a scripture to support it or explain it. My job was to find them.

In this book, each chapter has a scripture representing it, some at the beginning, some in the middle, but they all have a scripture at the end. I followed God's plan for me. I started writing chapter after chapter. Each chapter represents something different. I have written it my way. It is my hope that you, the reader, will be informed and entertained. In the reading of this book, you will learn and be able to understand the connection and significance of the basketball that's in my barber chair on the front cover of the book and how it made an impact on my life. You will share some happiness and sadness, and you will begin to think about the life lessons which are valuable learning tools for each and every one of us. Most of all, you will realize that in every event or situation, there is a lesson and a blessing.

~Matthew 5:16~
Let your light so shine before men, that they may see your good works, and glorify your Father which is in Heaven.

Dedication

I want to thank God for using me as a messenger in this writing. I am dedicating this book to my mother Jeanette Burnett, my father L. B. Burnett, and my brother Stanley Burnett, who are all deceased. I also dedicate this book to my wife and daughter who were so patient and supportive throughout this whole process. They are my everything.

Acknowledgements

I thank my brother Lynn for his faithfulness and hard work in managing Phase I Barbershop, and my sisters Faye and Tondra for their love and support. Although we did not grow up together, I acknowledge and thank my other siblings, sisters Mary Anderson, Tracey Cohen, Chaka Golightly, brothers London and Darrell Burnett, and Cadavius Casey for their love and support. I would like to thank my past and present long-time customers and their families and friends for allowing me to serve them over the years. Without all of you this book, *Behind the Chair,* would not exist.

I thank my staff of barbers and beauticians at Phase II Barbershop, Mel "Melo" Stevens, Keith "Keyboy" Crocker, Lecita "Kita" Porter, and Tondra "Cuz'n Emma" Scott, who are the best group of co-workers anyone could have. I extend my gratitude to Nikki Richards, photographer of ZnZ Photography for the cover photographs.

I also extend a special thanks to many ministers and friends for their prayers and support while I was in this process of writing and attempting to make *Behind the Chair* a reality: my Pastor Dr. M.

Behind the Chair

Keith McDaniel, Bishop Dr. Charles Jackson, Rev. Kaiser W. Jones Sr, Dr. Byron Corbitt, Rev. William Smith, Rev. Rosavelt Copeland, Rev. Sharome Gentry, Rev. Steve Watson, Rev. Ronnie Miller, author Bobby E. Mills, Ph.D., author Ms. Beatrice Hill, Mrs. Ella Long, and Mrs. Cynthia D. Jeffers, my writing consultant.

To my wife Sharon, I love you. I thank God for blessing me with you. You are my wife, my best friend, my soul mate, and you have always been that solid rock in my life. I am nothing without you. You are the wind beneath my wings.

To my daughter Talya, I thank God for giving us our perfect gift. The day you were born, you wrapped your finger around mine and then around my heart, and that was the best moment of my life. I love you with every ounce of breath in me.

~I Thessalonians 1:2~

We give thanks to God always for you all, making mention of you in our prayers.

Chapter One
The Barber's History

"These hands, engraved in the walls of this cave 20,000 years ago, may have been the first to cut human hair, or give it another shape different than the natural. The art of cutting or grooming hair is, undoubtedly, one of the most ancient arts in the history of mankind."[1]

According to the article "The History of Barbering" (thehistoryofthehairworld.com), barbers in ancient Egypt were distinguished and respected people. A statuette of Meryma'at, an ancient Egyptian barber, was found in a tomb in the lower cemetery of Thebes. Meryma'at lived over 3,300 years ago. He was responsible for shaving the Amun Temple priests. Every three days, the rite of shaving the entire body, face, and head was accomplished.

In ancient Greece, the profession of barber became very popular. Near the 5th century, men wore wavy hair and beards which were curled and combed. The first barbershops were thereby created in Greece. Much like today's shops, Greek barbershops became meeting places for men where they enjoyed reunions and long conversations about philosophy, politics, and community affairs. The article continues to explain how the hair was perfumed with scents made from flowers and olive oil.

Alexander the Great was also responsible for promoting the barbering profession. He was defeated by the Persians in several fights because his men had long beards. While in battle, the Persians would grab the beards of Alexander the Great's men, pull them off their horses and then kill them. As a result, Alexander the Great ordered all his men to shave their beards. The shaven look became popular and fashionable, thus creating more work for the barber. The men of these times visited their barber every three days.

~Job 12:12~

With the ancient is wisdom; and in length of days understanding.

Chapter Two
The Barber's Pole

The history of the barber pole is intertwined with the history of barbers and their bloodletting practices. Patients would tightly grasp a rod or staff tightly so their veins would show, and the barbers would cut open their arms and bleed them until they fainted. Later, when leech therapy became popular (they allowed for more controlled bleeding), leeches were applied directly to the vein areas.

After the procedure, the barbers washed the bandages, which were hung outside on a pole to dry, and to advertise the therapeutic specialties offered in the barbershop. Flapping in the wind, the long strips of bandages would twist around the pole in the spiral pattern we now associate with barbers.

This early barber pole was simply a wooden post topped by a brass leech basin. Later, the basin was replaced by a ball and painted poles of red and white spirals took the place of the pole with the bloodstained bandages, and these poles became permanent outdoor fixtures.

In fact, after the formation of the United Barber Surgeon's Company in England, barbers were required to display blue and white poles and surgeons, red ones. In America, however, many of the barber poles were painted red, white and blue.

There are several interpretations for the color of the barber pole. One is that red represented blood and white, the bandages. Another interpretation says red and blue respectively stood for arterial and venous blood, and white was for the bandages. A third view suggests that the spiral pattern represented the basin of leeches as well as the blood-collection bowl. Barbers' poles today are placed outside the shops revolving, and they are painted with red and white stripes with a ball on the top and bottom.

BARBERS and SURGEONS

Historically, barbers were also dentists and surgeons, versatile performers of tooth extraction and enemas, bloodletting and wound surgery. These barber-surgeons formed their first official organization in France in the year 1096, after the archbishop of Rouen prohibited the wearing of a beard. Later, as medicine became more defined as a field of its own, efforts were made to separate the academic surgeons from these barber-surgeons.

"In Paris, about 1210 A.D., identification of the academic 'surgeons as surgeons of the long robe' and the barber-surgeons as 'surgeons of the short robe' was established.

The Barber's Pole

In 1308, the world's oldest barber organization, still known in London as the 'Worshipful Company of Barbers' was founded."[2]

In an effort to systematically instruct barbers in surgery, a school was set up in France in the middle of the 13th century by the Brotherhoods of St. Cosmos and St. Domains.

> The guild of French barbers and surgeons established in 1391, and by 1505, barbers were allowed entrance to the University of Paris. The father of modern surgery, Ambroise Pare (1510-1590), was himself a common barber-surgeon before he embraced medicine and became the most famous surgeon of the Renaissance Period. Pare was a surgeon in the French army and was the chief surgeon to both Charles IX and Henri III. In England, barbers were chartered as a guild called the Company of Barbers in 1462 by Edward IV. The surgeons established their own guild 30 years later. Although these two guilds were merged as one by statute of Henry VIII in 1540 under the name of United Barber-Surgeons Company in England, they were still separated: barbers displayed blue and white poles, and were forbidden to carry out surgery except for teeth-pulling and bloodletting; surgeons displayed red and white-striped poles, and were not allowed to shave people or cut their hair.

Also, Louis XV of France decreed in 1743 that barbers were not to practice surgery. In 1745, George II passed several acts to separate surgeons from barbers. The surgeons went on to form a corporation with the title of "Masters, Governors and Commonalty of the Honorable Society of the Surgeons in London," which was eventually dissolved in 1800 during the reign of George III and replaced by the Royal College of Surgeons.[3]

The Bible contains several passages pertaining to the services of the barber. A few of the references may be found in the following:

- Deuteronomy 14:1, prohibiting shaving between the eyes of the dead.
- Leviticus 19:27, prohibiting trimming of the beard.
- Leviticus 21:5, prohibiting shaving the head.

  The greater part of the 13th chapter of Leviticus gives instructions for the diagnosis and treatment of diseases. In this chapter, the 29th through the 37th verses give instructions for the diagnosis and the treatment of scalp and face diseases by shaving and quarantine.
- In King David's time (1115-1055 B.C.) barbers played part in wars.

- In 595 B.C Ezekiel said: "And thou, son of man, take thee a sharp knife, take thee a barber's razor, and cause it to pass upon thine head and upon thine beard."

~Isaiah 7:20~

In that day the Lord will shave with a razor, hired from regions beyond the Euphrates (that is, with the King of Assyria), the head and the hair of the legs; and it will also remove the beard.

A blast from the Past

From left to right: Kimberly Palmer King, Gwendolyn Young Jones, Timmigo Burnett, Sharon Burnett

Phase II Barbershop

Owner Timmigo Burnett gives Wofford College
President Nayef Samhat a 'High on the side Skin Fade'.
Other operators: Mel Stevens, Keith Crocker, and Kita Porter.

Photo Courtesy of Mark Olencki at Wofford College

Fresh Cut

Master Barber and OJT Instructor Timmigo K. Burnett
gives his client Keondre Shippy a fresh haircut!

Chapter Three
The Black Barbershop

*B*lack-owned barbershops are more than just a place to get a shave and a haircut. Their position in American culture is well known, and the barbershop is a place where men can go and talk about events and ball games, and swap stories. According to author and Vassar College history professor Quincy Mills, the black barbershop allows African American men to become entrepreneurs. "During slavery and right after slavery, the black barbers exclusively groomed white men," said Mills. "They wouldn't even allow black men to get a haircut or a shave. White men didn't want to be shaved next to black men because it would signal a sense of formal equality."[5]

"The Black barbers in many cases were enslaved men, but also free blacks," Mills explains, "but barbering became a way for some African-Americans to find some little pockets to sort of figure out how they could at least earn a little bit of money, and control their time, which of course, was what the slaves did not have control over."[6]

The Black Barbershop

Some of the very first African-American entrepreneurs were barbers. African-American owned barbershops began to appear in the 1880s, 1890s, and into the 19th century. These shops, however, still reflected signs of a history of slavery serving wealthy, white clients such as politicians and businessmen. As more black men were born into a free society, more barbershops began to serve the African-American community.

At my barbershop, Phase II located at 300 Union Street in Spartanburg, S.C., we provide great service. We accommodate appointments and welcome walk-ins. The atmosphere is friendly, relaxed and pleasant. Our barbers and beauticians are confident and skilled enough to serve any ethnicity with any texture of hair. We respect everyone who patronizes our business; there are no drugs, smoking, drinking, cursing, gambling, or fighting. We do not engage in negative conversations about other barbers or barbershops in our community. Sure we have fun, joke, laugh, and share the latest news just like any other barbershop; however, we want our shop to be the kind of place where a family can come and be comfortable and feel respected. Along with great service, we want our customers to say, "We will be back." We have a pizza day for students going back to school. We also give free back-to-school haircuts for the young men who live at the local boys' home. Each year, we have a Customer Appreciation Day, and we offer free donuts every Saturday and a free breakfast several times a year to our customers.

Being a barber is a privilege, so I take pride in accepting the role as a mentor to our youth and a leader in our community. I also thank God for our predecessors in the barbers' profession, for they paved the way so that I (or we) could have the opportunity to be shop owners and entrepreneurs.

~Deuteronomy 11:31~

And it shall come to pass, if ye shall hearken diligently unto my commandments which I command you this day, to love the Lord your God, and to serve him with all your heart and with all your soul.

Chapter Four
Broken Home

I was number four of five children in my family. In those days, we were considered a large family. We lived modestly. We had two bedrooms, Mom and Dad in one and the five children in the other bedroom. Our room had a set of bunk beds and one full-sized bed. My brother Lynn and I slept on the top bunk, and my brother Stanley slept on the bottom. My sisters, Faye and Tondra, slept in the full sized bed. We were so close that we really understood what it meant to "reach out and touch." We had a thirteen-inch black and white television which showed channels four and seven clearly. Sometimes channel thirteen came in clearly if the aluminum foiled clothes hanger which served as our antenna was positioned just right. Unlike today, when the TV plays for twenty-four hours, after the 11:00 news broadcast, the TV announcer would say, "Do you know where your children are?" The TV stations would sign off completely after playing "The National Anthem." The screen would turn black: no movies, no videos, and no all-night flicks. It was lights out for us.

Behind the Chair

The mornings were always fun. If the milk was low, we would try to beat each other getting up in the morning just to get the last of it for our cereal. Even though times were supposed to be tough and the economy was supposed to be bad, I couldn't tell. We had food, clothes, a warm house, and we got gifts for Christmas just like any other family. In fact, when I was seven years old, I got a pony for Christmas. I had the cowboy boots with spurs, a hat, a gun and holster. I thought that I was the black Little Joe Cartwright who played on Bonanza.

Because we were so close and happy, it seemed that nothing was wrong, or that nothing could go wrong. Unfortunately, our house burned down a year later, and we moved from the country setting of Gilliam Town to the big city of Greer, South Carolina. By the time I was twelve, I was a child living in a broken home, but I didn't know it. In fact, I didn't internalize that until a few years ago. I just never thought of it that way. My parents were having problems and they eventually separated. When my dad was gone for about two weeks, I moved out to be with him. I wasn't choosing between my parents; I loved them both. I moved with my dad so that I would always know where he was. While with my dad, I still had both parents in my life. This was just the way it had to be at that time for me. That Christmas, I received a bicycle. After getting the bike, I moved back home with my mom. Although my parents were not in the same house, they communicated with each other, and both of them were always there for us. I'm glad that I didn't let my family situation define me, confine me, or label me a statistic.

I remember when my daughter was in the sixth grade, she came home and told us that some of her friends at school asked her if she lived with her mother or her father? She was confused; she didn't understand. She thought that all children lived with both parents. We explained to her that sometimes things happen between parents and they have to separate. I began to think about the number of programs available to single parents in today's society and especially those non-profits which are available to fathers. These agencies were not available to my parents; yet, they understood their responsibility and they still parented their children. We knew we were loved and supported by both of them.

My mom, dad, and my brother Stanley are living with God now, but I cherish those memories, and those memories come mostly when I'm behind my barber's chair. I think about the Christmas Stanley and I went to the woods to cut down a Christmas tree. My brother Stanley loved cars. He had four of them and they were all blue. I often remember when my mom's health was failing her, and she wasn't the same mentally or physically anymore. She didn't have to cook, clean, work, or pay bills anymore. All she had to do was be Mom. During those times, I would pick her up on my lunch break and we would go eat together. Sometimes, she just wanted to ride around town. You know, my mom only spanked me once. The only remembrance I have of the spanking is that it didn't hurt, but she set the standard of her expectations for me. She said that she didn't want to spank me, but she had to. She was a strong, beautiful woman, and she carried herself with a lot of pride. She worked in an office building cleaning them, but the way she dressed for work said, "I own this building."

When I'm behind the chair, I think of her most. When I was a child, she would come into the room in the middle of the night if I were sick and give me something to take. She'd put a rag on my chest and make things better. I miss her so much, and I'm forever grateful that she passed that affection on to me. When my daughter was younger, I'd go into her room to make sure that she was still breathing, and I do still do that.

When I think of my dad, I wish that I could tell him that I had accomplished all the plans that we talked about. I wish I could thank him for listening and for being there all the time. He was a man among men. When he said something, you listened. I'm not sure if everyone respected him that much, or if they were just afraid of him. He said to me, "Don't let anybody run over you!" Before he passed, I went to his church with him. The ushers were passing the collection plate. He leaned over and said to me, "Don't put all your money in the first time; they're coming back around again." I laughed. I thought about it later, and I believe that even though I was a grown man, Dad was still trying to teach me and make sure that I had money left for myself.

Seven years after my dad passed, I sang my first solo, "The Wind Beneath My Wings," at his church as a tribute to him. When I finished, I walked straight out the doors of the church. The congregation followed me. Tears filled my eyes. When I reached his grave, I said, "Dad, I did it." That's when I finally let go and accepted that he was gone.

I thank God for my parents. They each gave me something to hold on to. I believe in the Lord, and I know what the scripture says about death. However, when I'm behind the chair, I wonder if my mom, dad, and my brother know that I'm still here and that they have a family who loves them and misses them. I want them to see us, and then I think that although I come from a so-called broken home, I did not come from a broken family. I did not have broken parents. All that remains with me is love.

~1 Corinthians 13:13~

And now abide faith, hope, love, these three: But the greatest of these is love.

Chapter Five
My Foundation

*A*t this stage of my life, I have really come to know myself and my purpose. I know that God has the play book, and He can change the game plan at any time. When I'm behind the chair, I think about my early days. I remember wanting to be the best at everything I did. I was brought up in New Hope Baptist Church in Greer, S.C., and I sang on the children's choir. When I played marbles in the neighborhood, I wanted to win everybody's marbles. We climbed trees, and I wanted to go the highest in the tree. We threw rocks, and my goal was to throw my rock the farthest. When I got my PF Flyer tennis shoes, I thought that I could jump higher and run faster than any of my friends. One day, I was running and jumping over bushes and landed on a piece of glass, cutting my backside. I still have the scar today.

When I was seven, I broke my leg playing football. Actually, I was in the way of the big boys playing ball, and my brother Lynn fell on me and broke it. While I was in the hospital with a metal pin

My Foundation

through my ankle and my leg in traction, I got a pony for Christmas. My nurse's name was Mrs. Starlena. I liked her so much that I named my pony Star after her. At that time, it seemed cool to name my pony after her, but when I got older, I thought about it. Why did I name a horse after that lady? When I was ten years old, a pig had gotten loose in our neighborhood. About five of us chased that pig for two hours. I wanted to be the first to catch him. I caught him by his hind legs under a house full of chickens. Mr. June Mills, the owner of the pig, paid me five dollars which was lots of money forty years ago. I was dirty and had chicken mess all over me, but I was happy that I was the one who caught him. Around this age, I developed my competitiveness, the mentality of wanting to be first, wanting to win, or be the best regardless of the challenge.

I have always wanted to make my parents proud of me. I tried to stay out of trouble, make good grades, go to college, work hard, dress nicely, and do all the right things that would set me apart. It was important to me to hear my parents say that they were proud of me. My mother gave me character and taught me how to hold my head high. My dad gave me toughness and taught me how to work hard and be independent, and responsible. He told me to pay my bills on time and that I could have anything I wanted. I actually started working when I was ten. I collected bottles and sold them back to the store. I picked pecans and sold them door to door. When I was twelve, I made my first pay check. I cut grass with my Uncle Javan and got my first check for eighteen dollars. During the summer, I picked peaches for Dobson's Peach Shed, and at night I helped my dad clean offices at a mill. By the time I was in the ninth grade, I worked in a job's program during the summer. I worked at a middle school keeping the grounds up and getting the classrooms ready for the beginning of the school year. My junior and senior years in high school, I drove the school bus. After my junior year in high school, I worked at a manufacturing company welding with my Uncle Freddie. During the summer after graduating from high school, I worked at Fibers, Inc. I also played basketball while I was in high school.

I jogged the neighborhoods of Sunnyside and Greentown dribbling my basketball. As I would pass the houses of the neighbors, people like Mrs. Mary Mack, Mr. Verdale Richardson, and Mr. Porter Cox would shout out to me, "Keep dribbling that ball, Timmigo." Those shout-outs meant more than anything, and they inspired me to work even harder.

Mr. Doug Gregory, the owner of Gregory's Boutique in Greer, S. C. for over forty years, is the first successful black businessman and entrepreneur that I knew personally. He has been a mentor and friend to me. He has never been too busy to talk with me or share positive information about business or life. Those were words of encouragement to me. For four weeks prior to going to college, I used those basketball skills and worked as a counselor at Belmont Abbey College at a basketball camp while working part time at McDonalds. I didn't know it then, but I believed Philippians 4:13, "I can do all things through Christ which strengthens me."

My Foundation

Today I am a husband, father, businessman, and entrepreneur. However, before I could become a devoted husband, father, and provider with a thriving business, a foundation was laid for me. At the base of this foundation were determination and a strong work ethic. God placed a basketball in my hands, a coach, a team, and positive people in my life. I had a good start, and it has carried me into adulthood. Basketball was my safe place away from drugs, alcohol, smoking, and other things that trapped many of my peers. I still see many of them walking the neighborhood as if it were the seventies. Believe or not, some are still riding bicycles just as we did when we were younger. I give God the glory! It could have been me.

I truly believe that God and basketball saved my life. That's why the slogan on my basketball camp T-shirt is: God Saved Me! Basketball Raised Me! I had good parents, and they were there for me, but at a certain age, you must make choices and decisions. I would rather be on the basketball court than in the street getting in trouble or doing the things that captured some of my friends and others into addictions, prison, or death. My foundation helped prepare me for my life behind the chair. I encourage each of you to build on all that is good and Godly in your life. Make that your foundation.

~Jeremiah 29:11~

For I know the plans I have for you declares the Lord, Plans for welfare not for evil, to give you a future and hope.

~Psalm 11:3~

If the foundations are destroyed, what can the righteous do?

Chapter Six
Life's Work

*T*hrough our life's journey, we sometimes live for others more so than we live for ourselves. We make decisions based on what is best for others. We do things to impress or make others happy, and sometimes those for whom we do the most are the least appreciative and rarely acknowledge it. I believe that life is set before us like a test, a puzzle, or maze. We have everything within our reach, which has been given by God, for us to make it through life's trials, tribulations, heartaches and pains. The scripture proclaims, "But my God shall supply all your need according to his riches in glory by Christ Jesus," Philippians 4:19

As we navigate our lives, it's up to us to make the best of the journey. We must take care of our minds, our bodies, and our souls as God commanded us. We must find our purpose and develop our gifts. Whatever our purpose is or whatever our gifts are, we will find them in our life's work if we study His way and follow His map. Wherever we are today, it is where God wants us to be. We must seek God's face and make a conscience effort to be like Him. One may think that handling failures in life is tough, and that it throws stumbling blocks in your way. Some will be jealous or envious of your success instead of being happy for you, not understanding that if God has blessed you, he will bless them as well. Romans 1:10 says, "Making request, if by any means now at length I might have a prosperous journey by the will of God to come unto you." Those who have a good heart and are not selfish will do for others. It could be a family member, friend, or a stranger. My mother was like that. She fed people who were hungry. She gave the homeless a place to stay. I'm sure there were many times that she went without. God bless you, Mom.

~Philippians 2:4~

Look not every man on his own things, but every man also on the things of others.

While searching the internet, I found a great site of quotations from some noteworthy individuals on life and living. I hope you enjoy reading them as I did. I also hope that you will think about them and maybe make some adjustments in your living. They are as follows:

1. "How far you go in life depends on your being tender with the young, compassionate with the aged, sympathetic with striving, and tolerant of the weak and the strong. Because

Life's Work

---

someday in life you will have been all of these." **George Washington Carver** [7]

2. "Go forth today, by the help of God's Spirit, vowing and declaring that in life – come poverty, come wealth, in death – come pain or come what may, you are and ever must be the Lord's. For it is written on your heart. We love Him because He first loved us." **Charles Spurgeon** [8]

3. "In almost everything that touches our everyday life on earth, God is pleased when we're pleased. He wills that we be as free as birds to soar and sing our Maker's praise without anxiety." **A.W. Tozer** [9]

4. "Words can never adequately convey the incredible impact of our attitudes towards life. The longer I live, the more convinced I become that life is 10 percent what happens to us and 90 percent how we respond to it." **Chuck Swindoll** [10]

5. "Where I was born and where and how I have lived is unimportant. It is what I have done with where I have been that should be of interest." **D.L. Moody** [11]

~Psalms 23:4~

Yea, though I walk through the valley of the shadow of deaths, I will fear no evil: for thou art with me; thy rod and thy staff they comfort me.

Chapter Seven
Decision Time

~Proverbs 3:6~

In all thy ways acknowledge Him, and He shall direct thy path.

*I*n September of 1990, I enrolled in barber school at Lynn Wiley's Hair Styling Academy located in Greenville S.C. After working twelve years at Arrow Automotive, I decided that it was time for me to try and better myself and my family. At this point, my wife Sharon and I had no children. It was the perfect time for me to make that step. When I first considered going back to college, I was interested in becoming an electrician since I had become pretty good at installing ceiling fans and light switches. I felt that I was good with my hands. This was not my original plan, though. My plan was to come out of college and become a basketball coach. I thank God there was a ram in the bush for me. It is also ironic that I would choose barbering as a career. My brother Lynn is a registered barber, and my sister Tondra is a beautician. My dad was what you would call a shade tree barber. That's someone who cuts hair with no license. The shop that he worked in was located in the basement of the Sullivan Brothers Mortuary. The owner would allow my dad to cut hair there on the weekends, and he would primarily give my dad the customers that he didn't want to cut, like peach pickers and mill workers with cotton in their hair. I have learned that if you want to be successful in this business, you can't discriminate against anyone.

When I was in the 9th grade, I shaved the heads of about ten football players on my team for initiation. While in college, I would cut some of the guys' hair who were on the basketball team. I was not that good of a barber at that time, and I never even thought of barbering as a career. That's just how God works, though. He was setting me up for my blessings behind the chair. However, I had to go through a few obstacles first. Nevertheless, I was focused and determined to make the best out of this opportunity, and I knew that if I applied myself and kept the faith, it would work out.

There was one problem. I worked at the warehouse at the plant, and it was mandatory for us to work overtime to complete orders. Working those hours would not give me enough time to make it to class. I had a supervisor, however, who would let me off early so that I could travel about forty-five minutes to attend class. He insisted that he was not going to hold me back from trying to better myself. As I traveled back from school, I would stop and cut somebody's hair for practice or for gas money. Times were a little rough back then, so I thank God for guys like Jerome "Block" Johnson, Terry Brewton, and Larry "AJ" Briggs for giving me the opportunity, and not being afraid to be my guinea pigs. (After twenty-three years in this business, they are still my customers).

Before I enrolled in barber school, I would ride with my wife to work until payday. After payday, we would have enough gas money for both cars. While working at Arrow Automotive and attending school, I would often write on boxes and make plans. I would draw diagrams of what my barbershop would look like someday, and estimate how much income I could make. I daydreamed of being an entrepreneur and being my own boss. I also thought that if I made it out of the plant, I would not have to wear safety shoes, safety glasses, gloves, nor would I have to load a truck anymore and be freezing in the winter and hot in the summer. It took me about fifteen months to finish barber school. In September of 1991, two weeks before I finished school, my daughter Talya Shaniece was born. She was the miracle that changed my life! Our nurse said to us, "Take her home and enjoy her," and that's what we did. I would awaken her if she was asleep in the morning and kiss her before I left for work; I would awaken her when I got home from class at night. I wanted to see her eyes open, and I wanted her to see mine so that she would know her daddy.

I finished school and started my barbering career at a local barbershop named A-Cut for-U which later became BB&B although under the same management. I continued working at the automotive plant for another year before becoming a full-time barber. I got excited when we would get off early, or when we didn't have to work on Saturdays. Even though it had been a great place to work, there were always cut backs and layoffs that made you afraid to buy a new car, furniture, or purchase anything that would create an extra bill. As expected, the plant started the layoff process, but this time a layoff was a blessing. My supervisor actually asked me if I wanted to take the voluntary layoff. He said, "I understand what you are trying to do and this will be a good opportunity for you to test it." I took the voluntary layoff and was called back after five weeks; I had to make a decision.

Being young and unsure of my decision to leave this job, I called my dad for advice. He said, "Son, if you feel like you can make it, and it's what you want to do, I'm behind you."

The next person I called was my wife. She asked, "You don't want to go back, do you?"

"No!" I answered.

She said, "Well, don't go back. I'm with you; we can make it." With God on my side, and those two people in my life having my back and support, and now with a little baby girl depending on her daddy, that was all the confirmation I needed. I prepared a professionally typed letter, made copies and distributed them to about five people at the plant. The letters were distributed to the CEO, the plant manager, and all the supervisors, including my boss. Needless to say, I was a little afraid. I was leaving a place where I had grown up. It was like a family there, and I didn't want to burn any bridges.

I told them, *"Thank you for allowing me to work here for the past twelve years. I have enjoyed it. I was able to provide for my family, meet a lot of good people, and make a lot of friends. I will take all the work ethics, the dedication, discipline, principles, and memories with me. Thank you all, Warehouse & Friends."*

In November 1995, God blessed me with the opening of Phase I Barbershop in my hometown of Greer, S.C., and it is still operating under the management of my brother Lynn. This was an investment and a test of my ability to own a business. In March 2003, through much prayer and planning, God blessed me to open up Phase II Barbershop located in Spartanburg, S.C. Upon leaving the barbershop where I started, I thanked those at BB&B for giving me an opportunity, for allowing me to work there for twelve years and learn and grow there as well. I also thanked my devoted customers for their continuous dedication and support. I realize that there are plenty of other barbershops they could patronize, so I thank God for them.

Is it time for you to make a decision and make your dream a reality?

Decision Time

~Habakkuk 2:2-3~

And the Lord answered me, and said, Write the vision, and make it plain upon tablets, that he may run that readeth it. 3) for the vision is yet for the appointed time, but at the end it shall speak, and not lie: though it tarry, wait for it; because it will surely come, it will not tarry.

Chapter Eight
Inside Pain

*I*n each of our lives, there are situations that will be beyond our control. Things are not going to go our way or be in our favor. We are going to be disappointed. Our friends, family, and others will let us down. Even our goals, dreams, and blessings will be postponed, but we have to keep the faith and believe that God will see us through it all.

There are times that I reminisce about the beginning of my career as a barber. I must say that it wasn't an easy or smooth start. I had assumed that since I had worked at a plant with a lot of guys, I would have the opportunity to cut their hair. It was disappointing when it didn't happen. Sad and depressed, I called my dad and told him the situation. I was hurt and disappointed about them not giving me a chance. He told me not to worry about them because it was their choice and that I should move on. After that point, I was relieved and even more determined to make it work. Approaching it from a different prospective, I became an impersonator of a poker player, never letting anyone see my hand, or emotions. I developed the patience of Job, waiting, learning my craft, and perfecting my skills. I was working, smiling, laughing, and talking to these guys, but they never knew the inside pain that I was enduring. I found the strength and a calm place in the Lord that would allow me to get through that part in my life so that I would become who God wanted me to be.

~Isaiah 40:31~

… but they that wait upon The Lord shall renew their strength, they shall mount up with wings of an eagle, they shall run, and not be weary; and they shall walk, and not faint.

Without anger or hatred towards any of those who I thought were my friends, I was able to continue my career and not let this hinder my goal. Maybe they were my friends, but at that time it didn't feel like it. I assumed that friends supported friends. Eventually, I was able to service a few of them. I also had to realize that most of them already had a barber, and they could have just been loyal to their barbers, just as my customers. I was only seeking a chance and an opportunity to serve them. I'm neither bitter nor angry about that experience; in fact, I am thankful for it because it strengthened me, and it was a blessing and a lesson.

Behind the Chair

I've thought much about my blessing and lesson situations. One occurred when I put my faith in someone else. Once I spent my whole pay check on some wire rims for my 1980 280z. I got paid on Thursday and went to Rutherfordton, N.C. to get the rims that I had seen in a *Trading Post* newspaper. I went throughout the weekend with no money, but my car was looking good and I was happy. On Monday, I had planned to ask a co-worker to lend me five dollars until pay day. I could have called my dad for sure, but at the age of twenty-four I was trying to be a man, an independent man. So, this guy was one who bragged about what he had and flashed his money all time. Surely, he would let me borrow five dollars. I finally asked him on Tuesday if he would lend me five dollars until the following Thursday. He looked at me and said he didn't have it! I was totally shocked, disappointed, and embarrassed all at the same time.

I was angry about that for quite a few years. I was young and didn't know why, nor understand why he would not lend me the money if he had it going on like he said he did. After that experience, I made up in my mind that I would never spend everything that I had on things that I wanted but didn't need, and depend on or expect someone else to bail me out. In fact, every pay day I would get five dollars' worth of quarters from the bank and save them to make sure that I would always have some extra money.

Inside Pain

~1 Corinthians 16:2~

**Upon the first day of the week let every one of you
lay by him in store, as God hath prospered him,
that there be no gatherings when I come.**

This was inside pain to me because I had to hide the fact that it hurt me, and I couldn't tell anyone that I had asked him to lend me money and that he had said, "No." I didn't understand then, but I do now. This was also a lesson that would stay with me, and would prepare me for behind the chair. I forgave him in my heart, even though he probably never knew how much this had affected me. What I realized was that if he bragged and flashed his money, it was his money to start with and he could give it to anybody he pleased. Maybe he didn't want to give it to me. It was his choice. *Or maybe he didn't have it to give.*

~Colossians: 3:13~

**Forbearing one another, and forgiving one another,
if any man have a quarrel against any: even as
Christ forgave you, so also do ye.**

Each One Teach One

Passing it on from Father to Daughter

Each One Teach One

Timmigo & brother Lynn Burnett (Phase I manager)
examine a pair of clippers

Chapter Nine
Each One Teach One

~Matthew 25:16~

But he that had received the five talents went and traded with the same, and made them other five talents.

~Matthew 25:17~

And likewise he that had received two, he also gained other two.

~Matthew 25:18~

He that had received one went out and digged in the earth, and hid his Lord's money.

The parable of the talents is one of my favorite parables. For me, this parable represents how I must use what God has given me to the best of my ability. I must prepare myself to serve God faithfully by using my finances and any other gifts that I have to bless others. When God blesses us, we should want to help or bless others. We shouldn't be selfish with our talents. We need to teach, or show somebody else. There is an old Chinese proverb that says, "Give a man a fish and you have feed him for a day. Teach a man to fish, and you have fed a man for a lifetime." Jesus said, "Follow me; I will make you fishers of men," Matthew 4:19.

We all should be willing to share our gifts: whether it's a skill, musical gift or just dancing for the Lord. For thirteen years I was a basketball coach, a mentor, and a teacher to children of all ages. The most rewarding position was teaching my daughter the fundamentals of basketball and life, and passing on to her and others the blessings God had given me. I am a Master Barber, and I also have an OJT (On the Job Training) Instructor's license. This means that I can train students who have at least a ninth grade education to become a barber, and they do not have to attend Barber School. These trainees can obtain a license as well. I have been an instructor for twenty of my twenty-three years of barbering. I am proud to have trained twelve barbers. I could have been selfish and hidden my talent like the scripture said in Matthew 25:17, not trained anyone, kept my gift, my talent, and all my blessings to myself, but I knew how much God had blessed my family and me. He blessed me so that I could be a blessing to others.

I realized that I didn't make it this far by myself. In fact, there is someone that I want to thank for helping me get started and for putting the desire in my heart to become a barber. This guy took the time to talk to me and tell me the ins and outs of the profession. He gave me the name of the Barber School I should attend and, after I enrolled, he came to the school and did a few free demonstrations. As I continued to go to Barber School, he would allow me to stop by his shop and watch him cut hair. He encouraged me and kept me motivated. He showed me how to take the line out of a fade, and how to utilize the station mirror to see what the naked eye could not see when it comes to a professional haircut. This was a man that God blessed with a gift. He tutored me and was not concerned about charging me, nor did he ask me to work in his shop. I finally had the opportunity to tell him thank you about two years ago. Other than my wife, I had never shared with anyone about how he affected my life. During that special moment when I told him, tears flowed from his eyes, and I just hugged him and said, "Thank you, man, for what you have done for me." Even though I have told him, I want to thank him once again in front of those who may read this book because he is the reason that I am behind the chair today. His name is Keith Wright from Spartanburg, South Carolina. Paraphrasing another old saying, I am giving Keith Wright his flowers while he can still smell them.

Some of those that I have trained have worked for me, and some of them own their shops today. I thank God for putting the right people in my life to help me along this journey. Once I thought that the only thing for sure was death, taxes, and my jump shot, but if you live long enough you, a family member, or friend will have trials and tribulations for sure!

In 2002, through much prayer and some tough love, I was able to train my brother. He had been on drugs for about twelve years. Having a brother, sister, or family member on drugs can be devastating to a family because it affects everybody. He could not keep a job because of his addiction; he could not pass a drug test. He once asked me for my urine so that he could pass a urine test. Of course, I said no. He was always trying to convince us that he was straight and clean, but then he would have a relapse and we would not see him for a few days or a few weeks. I would give him money from time to time, buy him something to eat, and I even helped him get an apartment once when he appeared to be clean, but it didn't last very long. I told him, "When you make a change in your life, you won't have to try and convince anyone; the change will show." I was hurt, disappointed, and tired of being used. I prayed to God that he would take over this situation because it was bigger than me. I didn't give up on my brother; I just gave it to God and let him protect and guide him through this terrible addiction.

After I was able to let go and let God, my brother came to me and asked if I would train him to cut hair. I told him yes, but he was still on drugs, dirty, and had very low self-esteem. Many years had passed by before he asked me that life changing question again. I told him that in order for me to train him, he would have to go to church, and that he could not be that same person he was at that time and work in my place of business. Each week he called me and asked if he could work that day, and each week I would ask him, "Did you go to church?" For two weeks straight, his reply was no, and my answer was no. The third week he called with the same request, and I gave him the same answer.

For the next two weeks he was angry with me, so I didn't hear from him. It bothered me that I didn't hear from him. I wondered how he was doing, and I always expected a bad phone call. Early one Monday morning before eight o'clock, I received a call from my brother. He asked once again, "Can I work today?"

I answered, "Did you go to church?"

"Yes," he replied.

My body shook and my mouth dropped, but I said, "Yes. Meet me at the shop!" As I traveled to the shop, I was thinking that God was making his moves, and he was using me as a vessel. I had to make the next move in order for my brother to make his next move. So I bought my brother some barbering tools and some clothes for church. As he continued to attend church and work on his skills as a barber, I began to notice a change in my brother. He smiled more, his clothes were always clean, and he became an usher at church. It was all in God's plan. I felt that if he went to church, God would save him, put the right people around him, give him confidence and a sense of pride and purpose. It is a true statement: He may not come when you want him, but he is always on time.

Fourteen years later, my brother is still clean and is a registered barber at Phase I Barbershop in Greer, S.C. He tells me that I'm his hero; I say to him right now, "No, Brother. You are my hero."

Maybe this story applies to you and a love one or to you and a friend. Remember, don't let a mistake or a bad decision define who a person really is. Not only must we show our God-given gifts and talents, we must teach our crafts or skills, and teach others while we still have an opportunity to do so.

I thank God that I did not bury my gifts or talents. I see now that it is only through sharing our blessings that we are blessed. I thank God that I was able to help my brother and others because somebody helped me, and God expects us to do the same.

~Proverbs 9:9~

Give instruction to a wise, and he will be yet wiser, teach a righteous man, and he will increase in learning.

Chapter Ten
The Ride to Work

For over twenty years I have been an early riser, using that early work ethic that was instilled in me. Each morning on my ride to work at Phase II Barbershop in Spartanburg, I listen to the soft music on the stereo. It's a quiet time with God for me. I often find myself saying, "Thank you, God." I wonder and ask, "Why me, God?" I feel very humble for what God has done in my life. In spite of all I have been through, dangers seen and not seen, mistake after mistake, God still blesses me anyway. While driving, I think about the times I've failed and I got back up, the times I was talked about, and the times people doubted me. I think about those who prayed for me, those who had faith in me, those who had my back, those who believed in me, and those who love me. It all makes sense to me now.

There are people who are against you, and those who are there for you. We really are propped up on both sides. God won't allow us to fall. Our enemies make us stronger without realizing it. I believe that God places enemies in our lives, as well as those who love us, so that we will have balance. Then we can see what was already there from the start. This revelation will draw us closer to him. When those around us see that we are being blessed, they will diminish our accomplishments, or they will praise us. When they praise us, we must praise God. When they diminish us, we must still praise God. By giving back to God what he has given to us, we come to understand that if God made the heavens and the earth, he has all power and authority to do whatever he decides to do. I encourage you to read Luke 20:43, Psalm 110:1, Matthew 22:44 and Acts 2:35.

Whether it was raining, sleeting, or snowing, God has allowed me to make it to work, stand behind the chair and start my day. Even though it is a small space, it's my arena. There can be twenty or more people in the shop, but I can isolate myself where it's just me or my customer and me and the presence of God. My mind can be where I want it to be, and I'm still able to focus on the haircut. Behind the chair, I'm on display before my customers. They are constantly watching the way I cut, the way I handle myself, and sometimes they count the money by the number of heads they see me cut. I know because I have done the same thing!

In the space that I occupy behind the chair, there has been happiness, sadness, peace, love, pain, and ups and downs. Behind this chair, I meet people from all walks of life. To some I'm just a barber, but to others I am a counselor or a good listener. I am what they need me to be at that moment. I wear many hats at work. There is no time for me to be selfish and only worry about my problems or my situation because I don't know who I will come in contact with that day, nor do I know the role I need to play at that time. Sometimes, my customers are lonely people who need someone who will listen and not judge or criticize them. Whoever God wants me to be or whatever God wants me to do, I'm going to do it. I must be ready for whatever my customers need. I once witnessed a customer sweating profusely. Tears were streaming from eyes while he was setting in my chair. I didn't say a word, and he never said anything either. I realized he didn't want me to know what he was going through. It is the nature of all of us to be selfish and want to put our own needs and desires before others. However, by helping others in need, God will bless us also. Every child of God should be willing to help out a co-worker, friend, child, family member, or stranger.

~I John 3:17~

But whoso hath this world's good, and seeth his brother have need, and shutteth up his bowels of compassion from him, how dwelleth the love of God in him?

There are times when I do feel like I minister to people, whether it's kids about school, sports, and life, or whether it's adults about jobs, finances, relationships, business, health and God. I think that my customers really value my opinion, and respect me as a person and their barber. This really encourages me to be the best person, husband, father, barber, and role model that I can be!

~Hebrews 6:10~

For God is not unrighteous to forget your work and labor of love, which ye have showed toward his name, in that ye have ministered to the saints, and do minister.

Chapter Eleven
My Success

*I*n the beginning of my career as a barber, I was excited, anxious, and afraid. I would go to hair shows, competitions and classes, and buy a lot of products and clippers to make sure that I was equipped with everything to be successful in this business. My goal was to go in with the attitude of becoming the best that I could be, and make plenty of money so that I could take care of my family, and that would make me successful. So, I put into practice all that I had learned from my parents, my teachers in high school and college, my discipline through sports, the experience through my past jobs, and of course the principles and skills that I learned in Barber School. I was blessed to have had positive people and positive influences in my life. This would nurture my success. The ethics instilled in me, and the discipline of working hard (starting work early in the morning and working late), enabled me to get established and create a clientele sooner, though it wasn't easy.

My Success

~Luke 12:48~

For unto whomever much is given, of him shall be much required.

Nevertheless, over the pass twenty-three years that I have been in this business behind this chair, I must say that it has been worth it, and a blessing to my family and me. For me, the meaning of the word "success" or "being successful" started to change as time passed by. Some people define success as having a lot of money, living in a big house, or driving a nice car.

As for me, I think that success is different for every individual. It depends on what your values, goals, and expectations are, and what your level of success is. I also think that you cannot be successful on your own. It takes the grace of God, hard work, dedication, and the love and support of others. If you don't have good people in your life, or those who want positive results in life, you find them ASAP. Negative people hold you back and block your blessings. I may not have fortune and fame, but I am successful because of the many people who have come into my life during my career as a barber. They humbled me, cared about me, and made me rich in my heart. The things that were so important or meant so much to me at the beginning of this journey of barbering don't mean the same anymore. The money and material things are not a major priority now. Sure, I like nice things, but I work hard every day so that I can take care of my family and other responsibilities because my wife and daughter depend on me and I'm not going to let them down. I take a lot of pride in being a good father, husband, and provider, which is what a man is supposed to do. I also work so that when someone is in need, I will be able to help.

One Saturday morning I cut a little boy's hair about ten years old and when I finished he paid me with eight dollars worth of nickels and dimes. I asked him, where did you get all this change from? He replied, "I've been saving it for my hair cut." I told him to put his change back in his pocket. At the end of the day, that is the joy of my success: being able to give back and bless someone else the way God has so richly blessed me. I am not perfect and no one is, but from the beginning of my career through the middle of it, God gave me favor. I was *saved* and He turned my life around and put something new in my heart. I found myself wanting to go to church regularly, tithing yand giving an offering and working in different ministries, instead of sleeping late on Sunday morning and then spending nearly all day washing and waxing my car before going to play a game of pickup basketball. A change had come at the right time, so that I could handle the blessings behind the chair. If I never cut another person's hair again, I can say that I'm successful.

My Success

~Acts-20:35~

I have showed you all things, how that so laboring ye ought to support the weak, and to remember the words of the Lord Jesus, how he said, *It is more blessed to give than to receive.*

~Joshua- 1:8~

This book of the law shall not depart out of thy mouth; but thou shalt meditate therein day and night, that thou mayest observe to do according to all that is written therein: for then thou shalt make thy way prosperous, and then thou shalt have good success.

Lost Communication

Left-Right Imir Kentrell Logan, Chandler Isaiah Leverett, Tennico Scott Porter, Raymond Gibbs III, Jason Hill, Ananiah Christina-Grace Miller, Antonio P. Chrisley

Chapter Twelve
Lost Communication

*B*ehind the chair I have seen the transition of times. There are no longer the traditional Saturday morning father/son or daughter sittings in the barbershop with the father talking and teaching his child important life lessons and reviewing situations that will be helpful to him or her someday. I have witnessed over the past few years parents bringing their children into the barbershop from toddlers to teenagers, and most of the time it's the mother who brings them. She has to play the role of both parents, with the father hardly ever present. This is an important time in young boys' and girls' lives that they are missing. As for the son, he doesn't get to receive important knowledge, information, or communication from his dad that he will need to survive as a young man. On the other hand, the mom (in most cases) does a really good job with her daughters, and the best she can with her sons. Although I respect and commend the mother for resuming the responsibility of a father, there are a lot of things that a boy cannot get from his mother about being a man. You have to communicate with them early and often to try and eliminate mistakes and bad decisions down the road, and a real father should be proud and honored to take on that responsibility.

There are some staggering statistics about our young men and women on a Wikipedia website:

Youth incarceration in the United States:

- In 2002 approximately 126,000 juveniles were incarcerated in youth detention facilities alone. Approximately 500,000 youth are brought to detention centers in a given year. This data does not reflect juveniles tried as adults. Around 40% are incarcerated in privatized, for-profit facilities. Also according to the Justice Department report released in July 2003, the U.S prison population surpassed the 2 million mark for the first time with 2,166,260 people incarcerated at the end of 2002.
- There were more than 10,000 inmates under the age of 18 held in adult prisons in 2002. The number of women in federal and state prisons reached 97,491. About 10.4% of the entire African-American male population in the U.S aged 25-29 was incarcerated, compared to 2.4% of Hispanic men and 1.2% of white men in that same age group. According to the report by the Justice Policy Institute in 2002, the number of black men in prison has grown to five times the rate it was twenty years ago.
- Today, more African-American men are in jail than in college. In 2000 there were 791,600 black men in prison and 603,032

enrolled in college. In 1980, there were 143,000 black men in prison and 463,700 enrolled in college.

- According to the National Association for the advancement of Colored People (NAACP), African Americans constitute nearly 1 million of the total 2.3 million incarcerated populations, and have nearly six times the rate of whites.
- In an August 2013 Sentencing Project report on Racial Disparities in the United States Criminal Justice System, submitted to the United Nations, One of every three black American males born today can expect to go to prison in his lifetime.[11]

With the progression of technology, the communication between parents and their children has gotten worse. Behind the chair, I have seen both of the parents come in, each one of them with a cell phone, an iPad, or a game device in his or her hand. Usually, their focus is on other things rather than talking or communicating with one another or their children. So, what we have is a missed opportunity to learn and teach children something that could possibly help them in the future. One word, one situation, or just the attention could be helpful in children's lives and keep them out of trouble, or even save their lives one day.

When my daughter was very young, we would sit on our steps and talk to each other. Even though she was only six or seven years old, I would tell her that this conversation was for when she was fifteen or sixteen. I wanted her to understand that it was a teaching and learning conversation for what (lies) ahead of her. That communication between us was developed early, and now she is in her fifth year of college at the University of South Carolina in Pharmacy School, and the closeness and the communication has not stopped. It was and still is my responsibility to prepare her in every way I can with the fundamentals of life.

Our children have an advantage because they learn technology early, but we need to also get back to investing time and imparting knowledge and wisdom into our children. Everything about life cannot be researched, googled, or read from a book. Social media has taken control of our young people as well as some of our adults. Whether you are black, white, or hispanic, we all need to be positive influences and role models in children's lives because they are our future, and communication is the key to their success.

~1Timothy4-12~

Let no man despise thy youth; but be thou an example of the believers, in word in conversation, in Charity, in spirit, in faith, impurity.

~Proverbs 22:6~

Train up a child in the way he should go: and when he is old, he will not depart from it.

Chapter Thirteen
Unnoticed Tears

Attending Barber School, learning different lesions, textures of hair, clipper techniques, and other such things will prepare you to be a barber, but it doesn't prepare you for other personal encounters that will come your way throughout life's journey. Each phase of your life will prepare you for the next, and you will grow in your expectations, your respect for others, yourself, your family, your community, and your faith in God. What this does is makes you humble, makes you want to do well and not let God, your family, or your community down. So, rather than only learning job skills like textures of hair or clipper techniques, you learn about how to love and care about others. When you have God in your life, it breaks your heart sometimes to see others suffer or struggle.

One of my customers called me one day while I was at the barbershop and asked for my help. He was having a difficult time. His wife was sick, he was unemployed, and their lights were about to be cut off. The power bill needed to be paid or it would be disconnected in the next four to six hours. If their power was disconnected, there would be a reconnection fee on top of the payment. This was a person who was full of pride and integrity, and it was extremely hard for him to ask me for help. He came into my barbershop, we went into my office, and we talked about it. As we talked, I could see tears rolling down his cheeks as if he had lost a loved one. There was no doubt that he was sincere and needed my help. So I gave him the money, and he promised that he would pay it back to me. I said, "Ok, just get yourself together before you leave out of the office." I didn't want anyone to see him in that way, nor did he.

Once he got into his car, I could see from the window that he was still crying with his head down. I went out to his car and told him, "I know that you said you would pay me back but if you do, it will set you back even further. So don't worry about paying me back. I'm just glad I was able to help you." He broke down even more. The tears that he cried turned into my tears once I got back inside the barbershop. He never saw those tears, neither did the next customer that I was about to cut. I thank God that I was able to help him. He had been a blessing to me, and I was glad that I could be a blessing to him.

~Matthew 5:42~

Give to him that asketh thee, and from him that would borrow of thee turn not thou away.

~John 15:12~

This is my commandment, that you love one another as I have loved you.

That was just one of the many situations that I have encountered. When God blesses you to be a blessing to others, it's not meant to be bragged upon or boasted about. It's only the blessings of God and you have to realize that the situation could very well be turned around. It could've been me!

There was another situation with a customer of mine that I have been serving for more than fifteen years. He was a strong, healthy, and hardworking man about fifty-four years old. On this day, I noticed that he was walking a little differently, but I didn't mention it because it could have just been my imagination. However, the next couple of times I saw him, his walk seemed to have gotten a little worse. Finally, he told me that about three months prior he had been diagnosed with multiple sclerosis, a disease that affects the brain and spinal cord resulting in a loss of muscle control, vision, balance, and sensations such as numbness. With multiple sclerosis, the nerves of the brain and spinal cord are damaged by one's own immune system. I really felt badly for him. Several months went by and he would come by, but his health was declining. He had to eventually quit work and go on disability.

Behind the Chair

Fast forward—it had been nearly three years, and on this particular day, I watched him from my window. He pulled up. As he got out of his car, I could see that he was really struggling. He was holding on to every structure outside to assist himself in making it to the door. Once inside, he held on to the wall and the snack machines trying to balance himself. I came from behind my chair and walked over to him, grabbed his hand and said, "I got you." I helped him to my chair. This was a proud man who was embarrassed by the way he walked and how his body was failing him. That day was very difficult for me. Once again, the tears came down without notice. As I cut his hair, I wiped away tears, and he didn't even know how I was feeling. The whole time I was thinking: *He is in this situation with his health, and he's still trying to make it to me.* Something like a simple haircut that I felt was so unimportant at that time and in his case, but it must have been important to him.

This was a testimony that really makes you thank God for your health and strength, and the activity of your limbs. *This could have been me.* God could take the strength in my legs, the ability of my hands, and everything that I need to be able to do what I love, and that is cutting hair and taking care of my customers and my family. When I help someone or see things such as this the unnoticed, silent tears come because I'm so thankful and blessed to be in a position to help and do something positive in others' lives. Now, when he comes to the shop, I go out to his and car and assist him inside, and I help him back to his car when he leaves.

~James 4:6~

But he giveth more grace. Wherefore he saith, God resisteth the proud, but giveth grace unto the humble.

~I Corinthians 12:26~

And whether one member suffer, all the members suffer with it; or one member be honored, all the members rejoice with it.

The unnoticed tears that I shed for those men are a reminder that tomorrow is not promised. You can be doing well financially one day, in perfectly good health, and in the twinkling of an eye your whole situation and life can change. Life does not discriminate. Whether young or old, it has no preference.

The youngest customer that I have who has made an impact on my life is the most courageous kid that I know. His name is Tron Foster. He loves sports: basketball, football, baseball. He loves them all just like any other young man. On November 27, 2007, Tron was outside playing football with his cousin, and he fell to the ground after running with the ball. He got back up and said, "I'm ok, I'm a big boy." So he continued playing. Two days later, he woke up crying saying that he leg was hurting. After a doctor's visit, his mother was told that he was having growing pains and that they will stop soon. On December 15, the pain had worsened, so after another visit to the doctor, it was recommended that he see a knee specialist. Upon viewing x-rays with a specialist, it was determined that he had a tumor the size of a golf ball in his femur bone. It was very dangerous and with any slight movement or fall his femur bone could break. Following a biopsy, the results showed that the tumor was cancer. After a year of chemotherapy, he was allowed to return to school with some restrictions. However, after two weeks of being in school, Tron slipped and fell, breaking his femur bone and was in a body cast for eight weeks. With total knee surgery that required a rod in his leg and continued chemotherapy after three years he was finally done; he was in remission.

On November 26, 2012, there was another unexpected challenge. When Tron went for his checkup, his blood work was not normal. Results showed that he had (AML) which is Acute Myeloid Leukemia which is mostly seen in adults, but can be treated with a bone marrow transplant. Studies indicate that the parents are rarely a match but, praying for a miracle, doctors tested both parents. When the results came back, the mother was a perfect match. Tron was transported to M.U.S.C in Charleston, and on February 14, 2013, he received his mother's bone marrow. He was placed in an isolated room for six months and remained there in Charleston for an additional six months for treatment before being able to return home. Currently, Tron is being treated for graft-versus-host disease (a complication that can occur after a stem cell or bone marrow transplant) which damaged his lungs and his skin. He also takes fourteen pills a day, continues chemo every two weeks, and uses oxygen for shortness of breath. Now, he is being treated and monitored for another knee surgery and a lung transplant.

~Luke 18:16~

But Jesus called them unto him, and said, 'Suffer little children to come unto me, and forbid them not: for of such is the kingdom of God.'

Behind the chair, watching this young man come in the shop, remembering how healthy he was and the change in his physical appearance the unnoticed tears, in this case, get exposed. This little boy has endured so much so young, and not once have I heard him complain or have I seen him shed a tear. As I cut his hair, I wonder what's on his mind. Does he ever think about what his life will be like: will he be able to play sports again, will his health allow him to finish school, or how long will he live? Those are questions that you really don't want to think about, and some you probably don't even want to know the answer.

About two years ago, I was cutting his hair and I noticed that he was a little weak and that he was not saying too much. As I turned around and looked at a picture of him, my wife, my daughter and me, my tears began to come once again. At that point, I was trying to stay behind him *help him?* Before I finished cutting his now thinning hair, I dried my eyes. I turned him around in the barber chair and got close to his face and looked him straight in his eyes, and I told him, "You have a lifetime of free haircuts." He looked at me as though he did not understand, and then I said, "You don't have to ever pay for a haircut from me again."

He then looked at me and smiled and said, "Okay!" That was a moment that I will never forget. He really is a strong and courageous kid. As I write this, the tears are not silent or unnoticed, but they are tears of joy.

~Psalm 56:8~

Thou tellest my wanderings: put thou my tears into thy bottle: are they not in thy book?

Chapter Fourteen
The Last Time and Phone Calls

I have had a lot of good customers sit in my barber's chair. I've made a lot of friends, shared a lot of personal and sensitive moments, and shared some ups and downs. While servicing clients and conversing with them, I don't have a clue if this will be our last time communicating or if we'll see each other again. If I don't see a customer, I usually think that the customer has re-located or just changed barbers.

Once I noticed that one of my clients had not been in the shop for a while. I also knew that he was a diabetic, so I figured that he was sick. After about two months, he came in on crutches. His leg had been amputated. He seemed depressed, but glad to be alive and up and around. I really felt bad for him, and I was very surprised to see his leg amputated. I couldn't imagine what he was going through. Chills went all through my body when I saw him come in like that. I just tried to lift him up. I told him to hang in there and that God was in control of everything. After about three weeks, he came back in the shop. This time he had a prosthetic leg and did not have the crutches that day. His spirit seemed to be a lot better, and he seemed to be adjusting very well. As I cut his hair, we talked about his new prosthetic leg and how he was learning how to use it. We talked about his health and about life. He also told me that even though his leg was gone, it still felt like it was still there. Nevertheless, he left with a smile on his face. He was in a good mood and happy to be driving again. I am sad to say, his sister called me two weeks later and said that he had passed. Once again a friend and faithful customer had left this earth, and I didn't think that two weeks prior would be the last time that I would see him.

~Matthew 24:44~

Therefore you also must be ready, for the son of man is coming at an hour you do not expect.

Over the years, I have had many customers to pass on. For some, I'd cut their hair and then give them a ride home. (You can't beat that.) Some were black, white, young, and old.

The most devastating were the deaths of three men. Their ages were twenty-one, twenty-four and thirty-six years old, and they all committed suicide. This was a time when I really had to pray. I often wondered what I could have said or done to save these men that I had known for years. However, I did not have a clue that their problems

The Last Time and Phone Calls

were that severe. I was shocked and in disbelief that this tragedy had happened. Why? They were gone too soon, and I never got a chance to say good bye.

As I searched the Bible for answers about whether you go to Heaven or Hell if you commit suicide, I could not find my answer. I don't understand why these young men would take their lives and leave their families and friends with no reason or explanation. During my research, I did discover that there were seven individuals in the Bible who committed suicide and the reasons were documented. In Matthew 27:35, Judas committed suicide because of his greed and guilt after he betrayed Jesus. In 1 Kings 16-15:20, Zimri committed suicide by burning himself for the evil sins he committed and he did not want to face the consequences. In 2 Samuel 17:14-23, Ahithophel committed suicide because he felt rejected; his family and friends stopped believing in him. In 1 Samuel 31:1-6, Saul committed suicide in time of battle because he felt defeated.

In 1 Samuel 32:5-6, Saul's armor bearer committed suicide because he was fearful of being captured. When he saw that Saul was dead, he fell on his sword and died himself. In Judges 16:23-31, Samson committed suicide (indirectly) and willingly to get revenge on the Philistines; he laid his life down to save God's people. In Judges 9:50-57, Abimelech committed suicide because of arrogance and pride. So what this tells us is just because we don't know the reason, nor have an explanation, those who commit this devastating act feel they have reasons.

~John 5:28-29~

Marvel not at this; for the hour is coming, in the which all that are in the graves shall hear his voice, and shall come forth; they that have done good, unto the resurrection of life; and they that have done evil, unto the resurrection of damnation.

Phone Calls

Behind the chair, I serve my customers, handle business situations, and make business decisions. The phone rings a lot. People call to make appointments, telemarketers call to sell things. This is expected every day. Those calls are just calls that I address and then go about my daily business, and really think nothing of it. Then there are some calls of joy and good news like the birth of a new baby, someone getting married, or winning the game the night before–things like that.

Then there are other calls that you wish you hadn't received. The bad news comes like someone was in an accident, had a heart attack, got shot, or went to jail. I will never forget an early Saturday morning when my best friend Mundy Woodruff called me at work about 5:30 A.M. and said, "I need you, man." At first, I thought he was talking about a haircut, and then I remembered that I had just cut him on Thursday. I could tell in his voice that something was wrong. With a deep sigh he said, "My son got killed last night!" He started crying over the phone, and I started to cry. I felt bad for him and his family.

The Last Time and Phone Calls

I had been cutting his son Tay's hair since he was about six years old. He had turned nineteen that night at 12:00, and by 1:00 A.M. he was pronounced dead.

I received another phone call around 11:30 A.M. on a Friday pertaining to one of my customers who was riding a motorcycle. A car pulled out in front of him, and he died at the scene. He was a thirty-four year old man with a wife and daughter, family, and friends. He also was a long-time, faithful customer. I started cutting his hair when he was fourteen years old. His name is Brain Wofford and he had an eleven o'clock standing appointment every Tuesday. Three days after getting his hair cut, he was gone. Another one of my customers and good friend Pastor William Smith's son Matthew was in an accident as he had pulled over on the highway to secure his motorcycle and was struck and killed by a passing truck driver. This phone call also turned a good day into a sad day, but time heals and now when I talk to this man of God about his son he smiles as his son's name comes from his lips.

I have had the privilege of cutting the hair of many of my customers and relatives at the mortuary. The first deceased person that I cut was my father. I have to admit that I was scared, and I didn't know whether I would break down, cry, or whether I could even do it. Once I was in there and I saw my daddy, it was easy. I said to myself, "This is my daddy." I looked at him and began to feel his body all over. As I started cutting his hair, I felt proud to be in this profession and to be able to do this for my daddy. I also remember saying, "If I don't do this, I will regret it for the rest of my life." Some opportunities may be the last.

~Deuteronomy 31:6~

Be strong and of good courage, fear not, nor be afraid of them: for the Lord thy God, he it is that doth go with thee; he will not fail thee, nor forsake thee.

Chapter Fifteen
We Are all Handicapped

From behind my chair, I see people with different occupations from all walks of life: young, old, rich, poor, happy, sad, healthy, and sick. The truth is that we all have had those moments in our lives where we wish we could change something about us, or our lives. If we could only be the eyes behind the person that we think we see, we would see things from a different perspective; we would see and feel the happiness, the sadness, the pain, success and the failure that they feel. We would be surprised to find out that some people are not satisfied with the way their life is going and some people are not satisfied with qualities about themselves. God made each and every one of us different; however, we are all made in his image. We all have a handicap or deficiency. In our minds, it may seem to be a great problem; but in someone else's, it could be mute. There is a story that was told about a man who was searching for his socks, and he became very upset because he could only find one of the same pair, so he had to wear mismatched socks. He was angry, until he saw a man who had no feet. It was at that time he realized that he was complaining about something that was so small, and it didn't even compare to the problem the other man had.

The problem we have is that we complain, we stop, give up, or hide because we have a type of handicap or disability, and believe that we can't be successful or productive and can't be used by God. You don't have to be perfect; God can use you whether you're short, tall, have one leg or no legs, are hump backed, homeless, can't read, can't write, have a speech impediment, are blind, a back slider, or a non-believer. You can choose any one of those you want, and you put them in any order and God can turn a handicap into a miracle — your loss into your victory. The Lord gave a donkey the ability to speak. "…What have I done to thee, that thou hast smitten me these three times?" It asked Balaam (Numbers 22:28).

The Apostle Paul was described by Walt Wangerin as a small man sitting cross legged ...eyebrows thick and dark and joined in the middle; his nose both narrow and hooked; his eye red-rimmed in that tremendous skull; a swift mouth, moist red lips...an orange worm of a scar at the hairline. We can see in this description of Paul that he was not a very good looking man, was not made perfect. He also had some handicaps, but he preached the same gospel that Jesus preached, the Kingdom of God.

We Are all Handicapped

~ 2nd Corinthians 2:12~

Furthermore, when I {Paul} came to Troas to preach Christ's gospel, and a door was opened unto me of the Lord.

God has opened many doors for us all – from poverty, from disabilities, or from mental and physical challenges. James Earl Jones, a famous actor whose parents separated before his birth, was born in 1931 on January 17th (which is my birthday). As a child, he stuttered severely, which he overcame during his high school years. Before then, he was terribly self-conscious and shy around other children. He refused to speak in school until his English teacher helped him out of his silence. Jones later told a reporter, "He looked at a poem I wrote and said, 'It's too good for you to have written, so to prove you wrote it, please stand up in front of the class and recite it from memory,' and I did it without stuttering."[13] Jones went on to attend the University of Michigan to study medicine, but soon discovered acting. He would later be famous for his distinguished voice, and as a result has received numerous awards.

Stevie Wonder was another pioneer and innovator in the music industry who was born with a disability. He was born May 13th in Saginaw Michigan. Stevie Wonder was born blind. Even with this disability, he was able to grow up playing various instruments such as the piano, harmonica, drums, and bass. Stevie never participated

Behind the Chair

in many outdoor activities; however, he was a member of the church choir. At the age of eleven, he was given the stage name Little Stevie Wonder because many people were astounded by his ability to play numerous instruments and sing at the same time, and people called him Stevie, "A Little Wonder."

As I stand behind this chair, I see a variety of people who have health problems. Some can't walk that well, can't see that well, and some complain about this and that but never try and do anything differently. The doctor tells them to do one thing, but they do another. I hear the same story week after week. However, there are those who come in and never complain. They are walking with a cane or maybe just had surgery, but they still have a smile on their faces, and they are thanking God for a portion of their health and strength. They are just glad to be here. I had a friend that was confined to a wheelchair since birth. He was an independent person, clearly handicapped and disabled, but he didn't want to be treated that way. For years he maintained a steady job, lived by himself, caught the city bus, or just traveled on his motorized wheelchair to make it to his destination. This man refused to give in to his limitations. He used what God allowed him to use and didn't complain. He was at church every Sunday, sang in the male choir, and was also an usher. Sadly, my friend passed away April 24th 2011, but he left a huge print on my heart and on the hearts of many others who knew him, including those who have disabilities. His name was Donnie Collins.

We Are all Handicapped

~Philippians 4:13~

I can do all things through Christ who strengthens me.

In this chapter, we talked about individuals that have or have had some type of physical or mental disability. What we didn't talk about was our spiritual disability. I am a witness to the fact that I haven't always known the Word of God. I didn't go to church every Sunday; I never went to Sunday school or Bible study. I believed in God, but I did not read the Bible for myself. I only knew what the preacher said. So I was living a life of not knowing, missing something, not equipped. I believe that if we don't seek knowledge through the Word of God, we are limiting ourselves, and we won't be prepared when the enemy attacks us. We will be disabled because of the lack of knowledge and disabled because we won't have the ability to help others or lead others to Christ. I believe that a student of the Bible should know the difference between the Old and New Testaments. A student of the Bible should be able to recite the Ten Commandments. I believe that a person seeking to live like Christ should be able to share the plan of salvation.

~2 Timothy 2:15~

Study to show thyself approved unto God, a workman who needeth not to be ashamed, rightly dividing the word of truth.

~John 3:16~

For God so loved the world that he gave his only begotten Son, that whosoever believeth in him should not perish, but have everlasting life.

~Romans 10:9(NLT)~

If you confess with your mouth that Jesus is Lord and believe in your heart that God raised Him from the dead, you will be saved.

~Romans 3:23~

For all have sinned, and come short of the glory of God.

Chapter Sixteen
After the Program/After the Benediction

*I*n this particular chapter, God gave me a personal vision of the prodigal son and how it is also a part of our society. We find the parable of the prodigal son in Luke 15:11-32. I like this story because it speaks to what happens to people when they don't consider the consequences of their actions.

In summary, Jesus tells the story of a man with two sons. The younger son asks his father to give him his portion of the family estate. Once received, the son promptly sets off on a long journey to a distant land and begins to waste his fortune on wild living. When the money runs out and the son finds himself in dire circumstances, he takes a job feeding pigs. He is so destitute that he even longs to eat the food assigned to the pigs. This scripture clearly describes an immature, selfish young man with no plans, goals, or respect for his inheritance. He had no patience, he was in a hurry to get out into the world and not be under the guidance of his father, which was something that he needed to help him survive, but he didn't realize it until *after* he had spent all his money. However, God wants us to understand and appreciate his father's attitude. It is our responsibility to welcome the lost and rejoice when they return home.

I often go to recreational centers during the summer prior to my basketball camp which takes place in July and speak to youth between the ages of five and twelve. One of the main topics that I speak about is "After the Program." I try to get them to understand the importance of doing their best, listening, learning, and getting all the knowledge and discipline they can to prepare them for what happens after the program and for what happens in life. The majority of the participants don't realize that the program is about to be over. I tell them that at some point the teachers, the principal and staff have completed their assignments with you, and it's over now. There is no more sending you to the office, there are no more phone calls to your parents, and being the class clown is not an option anymore. They have put up with you long enough. Some will miss you, and some will be glad that you are gone. The teacher has taught, the bell has rung, and the class is permanently dismissed. The program is over, and now the questions remain: Are you prepared? Did you do your best? What are your goals, what are your plans? Are you ready?

The one thing that you don't want to have to say is, "I wish I had." "I wish I had paid attention, I wish I had listened to my teachers and my parents." Or, "If I could do it all over again, if I had just one more year, I would do things differently." Some people make that statement soon after, and some make it later on in life after they have made bad choices and decisions, just like the prodigal son. Sometimes, sharing your mistakes with your children, family or friends impacts their lives and decisions in a positive way.

~Proverbs 22:6~

Train up a child in the way it should go: and when he is old, he will not depart from it.

~Proverbs 3:6~

In all thy ways acknowledge him, and he shall direct thy paths.

For me, the prodigal son represents a person living in rebellion to God. Sometimes, we have to hit rock-bottom before we come to our senses and recognize our sin; but God waits patiently, with loving compassion to restore us when we return to him with humble hearts.

The benediction, a short invocation for divine help, blessings, and guidance, is usually at the end of worship service. After the benediction, we are dismissed from worship. I feel that even though the main and primary purpose for church is to win souls and bring people to Christ, we also have to receive and digest the sermon so that after the benediction, we can utilize the principles of God's Word in our lives, so that we will make the right choices and decisions. Not only does it affect us, it affects our family and those around us. Outside the walls of the church, the devil is on our backs seeking to destroy us. We need to understand that a person doesn't have to be in the church to be saved, and when a sinner is saved, we should rejoice just as the father of the prodigal son did when his lost son found his way home. Romans 10:9 says that if you confess with your mouth that Jesus is Lord and believe in your heart that God raised him from the dead, you will be saved.

It doesn't matter what a person has done, where a person has been or what sin a person may have committed, God saves sinners. In fact, in the book of Acts, Paul — a great missionary who wrote many of the letters in the New Testament — was a murderer. He once persecuted those who believed in Jesus. Paul is also a powerful example of how it is not impossible for God to reach and change anyone. I challenge you, the reader, to focus on your decision making after the benediction when you attend your next worship service. Also, while reading *Behind the Chair*, I pray that there has been something meaningful and helpful that will bless the heart of the reader and bless the reader's life in a positive way. God bless the reader.

After the Program / After the Benediction

~2nd Corinthians 5:17~

Therefore if any man be in Christ, he is a new creature: old things are passed away; behold, all things are become new.

~Jude 1:24-25~

Now unto him that is able to keep you from falling, and to present you faultless before the presence of his glory with exceeding joy, to the only wise God our Savior, be glory and majesty, dominion and power, both now and forever.

"Little Did I Know"
(A Tribute to my Coach)

It takes more to being a coach than just X's and 0's (I mean to be a great coach).

Even though he was the only one, basketball wise, I could literally see eye to eye. He was a big man to me.

Throughout the three years that I played for Coach Gooden, he was a coach, friend, and sometimes a drill sergeant. Yes, to be good, we had to run, but I have always looked up to him and respected him, and I always will.

In spite of all the coaching, teaching, directing, and disciplining, I didn't know that this was really setting the stage of building character in me for my life. We laughed and cried together.

Little did I know that something as small and simple as a basketball would play a major role in my life.

"Little Did I Know"

Litatle did I know that the emphasis on being at practice on time was preparing me for that job later on.

Little did I know that leaving my best on the court would influence me to give my best at everything that I do.

Little did I know that giving an assist would discipline me to share with others and not be selfish.

Little did I know that not caring who got the MVP would prepare me not to be jealous or envious when others are blessed.

Little did I know that Coach telling me to keep shooting would give me the confidence to know that if I fail once, I should try again.

I didn't realize that the coaching, the teaching, and the learning would continue after basketball.

All of these things may not mean much to you, but it really helped to mold me as a young man. I am blessed to have someone to catch me early and care about me as a person as well as a basketball player.

*He is a Father Figure.
*He is a Role Model.
*He is my Friend.
*He is my Coach.

THANK YOU, COACH MELVIN GOODEN!

~Proverbs 24:5~

A wise man is full of strength, and a man of knowledge enhances his might.

A Poem for My Bride

That night I saw you in that RED DRESS, out of all the girls there. You looked the BEST.

I asked for your number, and if you didn't mind. You said, "OK," but you took your own sweet TIME.

I came to your house as we started to date. Our first walk was to the Beacon where we stopped and ATE.

Not a day passed by that I would not call. And you were at every game when I played BASKETBALL.

After three years of dating, which wasn't my plan, I had fallen in love with a girl from HIGHLAND.

We got married, had ups and downs, good times and bad times, but our bills were paid even if it took our last DIME.

We knew something was missing in God's great world, so he blessed us with a beautiful baby GIRL.

If I haven't been the best husband, father, or provider you wanted me to be; maybe this time around, I WILL BE ALL THREE.

We made it through the rain, storm, and all kinds of weather. Our dream has always been to grow old TOGETHER.

We've shared laughter, we've shared tears, but I'm truly blessed to have YOU for the last 25 YEARS.

So here we are at the altar AGAIN, you're still my WOMAN and I'm still your MAN.

I LOVE YOU ALWAYS

TIMMIGO 9/22/09

~Mark 10:9~

What therefore God has joined together, let not man put asunder.

Bibliography

"The Barber Pole," *Encyclopedia Britannica*. (Chicago. William Benton, 1968). Vol.3 pages 148-149 and 327-328.

Carver, George W. – American Scientist. **brainquote.com/quotes/ author/george washington carver html**. June 6, 2014

Mills, Quincy T. *Cutting Along the Color Line: Black Barbers and Barbershops in America.* University of Pennsylvania Press, Inc. Oct. 24, 2013.

Standardized Textbook of Barbering Fourth Edition. Associated Master Barbers and Beauticians of America. 1950.

"Statistics of incarcerated African American males" – Wikipedia. org/wiki/Statistic.

"The History of Barbering". thehistoryofthehairsworld.com/barber-history.html

http://www.whatchristianswanttoknow.com/ 20-popular-bible-verses-about-life/#izz34UlUr9lo

End Notes

[1] "Cleaning services and staying for the head and..." Barber's History. March 3, 2014. thehistoryofthehairsworld.com/barber history.html.

[2] "Barber History." Barber Pole. Word information. 3 March 2014. wordinfo.info/unit/3364/:p.17.

[3] "Barbers and Surgeons." Barber Pole. word information. 3 March 2014. Thehistoryofthehairsworld.com/barber history.html.

[4] "The Bible Containing Passages." History of the barber profession. 7 April 2014. http://webpage.charter.net/bobbyrutledge/history%20of%20barbering.htm.

[5] Quincy Mills. "A History of the African-American Barbershop." *The Black Barbershop*. Interview with Kai Ryssdal. January 28, 2014. www.marketplace.org/topics/economy/history-african-american-barbershop. Accessed 9 May 2014.

[6] Ibid., 9 May 2014

[7] George W. Carver – American Scientist. brainyquote.com. 6 June 2014. www.brainquote.com/quotes/author/george washington carver html.

[8] Charles Spurgeon. "Quotes on the Holy Spirit". Go forth today, by the help of God's Spirit. 6 June 2014. www.godwithyou.org/charles-spurgeon.

[9] A. W. Tozer. "In almost everything that touches our everyday life on…" 6 June 2014. www.quotes.net/quote/50832.

[10] Chuck Swindoll. "Words can never adequately convey the incredible". Brainyquotes.com 6 June 2014. www.quotes.net/quote/52936.

[11] Dwight L. Moody. American Evangelist. "Where I was born and where I have lived…" 6 June 2014. mobile.brainyquote.com/quotes/quotes/…

[12] "Statistics of incarceration of African American Males". Sentencing Project Report. 15 July 2014. en.m.wikipedia.org/…statistics.

[13] James Earl Jones. October 16, 2013.en .m.wikipedia.org/wiki/jamesearljones.

About the Author

Timmigo K. Burnett is a Master Haircare Specialist and OJT Instructor with twenty-three years of experience in the barber profession. He is the owner of Phase I Barbershop located in Greer, South Carolina and Phase II Barbershop located in Spartanburg, South Carolina. He is a member of the 1978 Greer High School State Championship basketball team. He also founded The Total Package Basketball Camp in 2002. He is a proud member of Macedonia Missionary Baptist Church located in Spartanburg, South Carolina and is now the author of his first book, *Behind the Chair*. He resides in Moore, South Carolina with his wife Sharon and daughter Talya.

Our Family

*From left to right.
Sharon, Timmigo, and Talya.*

~Joshua 24:15~

But as for me and my house, we will serve the Lord.

CPSIA information can be obtained at www.ICGtesting.com
Printed in the USA
LVOW06s2233270715

447793LV00001B/2/P